VOICES IN THE NIGHT

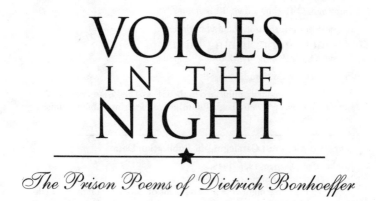

VOICES
IN THE
NIGHT

The Prison Poems of Dietrich Bonhoeffer

EDITOR AND TRANSLATOR
EDWIN ROBERTSON

ZondervanPublishingHouse
Grand Rapids, Michigan

A Division of HarperCollinsPublishers

Voices in the Night
Copyright © 1999 by Edwin Robertson

Requests for information should be addressed to:

📖 Zondervan Publishing House
Grand Rapids, Michigan 49530

First American Edition, 1999.

This book was originally published in the UK as *The Prison Poems of Dietrich Bonhoeffer* in 1998 by Eagle Publishing, an imprint of Inter Publishing Service (IPS) Ltd.

Library of Congress Cataloging-in-Publication Data

Bonhoeffer, Dietrich, 1906–1945.
    [Nächtliche Stimmen. English]
    Voices in the night : the prison poems of Dietrich Bonhoeffer / editor and translator Edwin Robertson.

        p. cm.
    ISBN 0-310-22874-3 (alk. paper)
    1. Christian poetry, German.   I. Robertson, Edwin Hanton.
II. Title
PT2603.062N3313 1999
831'.912—dc21
                                              99-29099
                                                    CIP

This edition is printed on acid-free paper.

Quotations from Bonhoeffer's letters are taken from:
1. LPP: *Letters and Papers from Prison*, The Enlarged Edition (London: SCM Press Ltd., 1971).
2. LLC 92: *Love Letters from Cell 92* (London, Harper and Collins, 1994).
3. There are three short quotes (accredited in the text) from J.C. Hampe: Hampe: *Prayers from Prison* (London: Collins, 1977). (Pp. 81, 91, 107 of my manuscript)
4. There is a short quotation, also accredited in the text from the introductory essay by the editor, from a letter from Otto Dudzus to Bonhoeffer: Dudzus, I: *Predigtn, Auslegungen, Medtationen, Chr* (Munchen: Kaiser Verlag, 1985).

All rights reserved. No part of this publication may be reproduced, stored in a retrieval system, or transmitted in any form or by any means—electronic, mechanical, photocopy, recording, or any other—except for brief quotations in printed reviews, without the prior permission of the publisher.

Interior design by Sherri L. Hoffman

Printed in the United States of America

---

99 00 01 02 03 04 05 /❖ DC/ 10 9 8 7 6 5 4 3 2 1

Acknowledgements

The preservation of the documents we owe to Eberhard Bethge and his wife, Renate. They have also kept alive their memories of Dietrich Bonhoeffer. In preparing these new translations of the poems, I have greatly profited from visits to Sabine, twin sister of Dietrich, and her daughter, Marianne Leibholz. The accuracy of the translations has depended upon constant consultation with Prof. Dr. Christian Gremmels, chairman of the German section of the *Internationale Bonhoeffer Gesellschaft*. Every draft of the translation has been sent to him and twice I have discussed at length with him in the warm hospitality of his home in Reinhardshagen, thanks to the care of his wife, Doris. I am grateful also to those who have listened to my reading of the poems aloud to assure that they sounded right as well as being accurate. In Hampstead, I must add a special thanks to the mixed group who came to my church on Thursday evenings and discussed at length each poem as I worked through them. Hampstead itself is a very unusual place. Its constituency includes many German-speaking people, both Jews and Christians. All have generously given of their time to help me bring a dynamic equivalent to my translations. But ultimately, none of these can be held responsible for the final result. Thanks is also due to those who have given permission to quote from printed material in the commentaries.

I owe much to the careful treatment of this book by David Wavre, my publisher, and his patience with my typing.

—Edwin Robertson

Contents

A PERSONAL NOTE

More than fifty years after his execution, the writings of Dietrich Bonhoeffer continue to influence, trouble, and disturb the church. For me this influence has been personal.

A few weeks after the end of the war, I attended a memorial service to a German I did not know in Holy Trinity Church, Holborn. There I heard the story of a remarkable German pastor who persistently risked his life to oppose the monstrous tyranny of National Socialism in Germany itself. George Bell, the bishop of Chichester, told of a bold step taken to bring the war to an end in 1942. It was impossible not to be fascinated by a German patriot who acted as a double agent in order to overthrow the government of his country in a time of war.

I was already beginning to make contact with German prisoners of war who were in the neighborhood of my church in St. Albans. With the help of the Bishop of St. Albans, Philip Loyd, we formed a fraternity of clergy and ministers, including Lutheran ministers in the neighboring camps. One of them, the Revd. Paul Schliebitz from Silesia, gave me a copy of *Das Zeugnis eines Boten (The Witness of a Messenger),* a booklet published by the

Ecumenical Commission for the Pastoral Care of prisoners of war in Geneva, December 1945, in memory of Dietrich Bonhoeffer. It was only 58 pages long and contained all I needed to know about this man at that time. It included essays by people who had known and lived with Bonhoeffer, some of his letters from prison, extracts from his published works, and some of his poems: "Voices in the Night," "Christians and Others," "Who am I?," "The Death of Moses" (an extract), "New Year 1945," and, in the introduction, a quote of the last "Stage" on the way to freedom, "Death." For me it was the path into a new world and for more than fifty years I have not been able to escape the influence of this man.

In 1947, I went to Germany to join the British Control Commission in Germany, with special responsibility for Religious Affairs. For two and a half years I lived and worked with people who had known Bonhoeffer—Praeses Koch, Hans Lilje, Martin Niemöller, Otto Dibelius, Klaus von Bismarck, and many others. They remained my friends as long as they lived.

In 1949, I left Germany to take up the post of Assistant Head of Religious Broadcasting at the BBC. This involved work with the producers of the Third Programme and very soon these German friends were broadcasting their experiences of resistance in Nazi Germany and their memories of Bonhoeffer. It became clear to me that his writings in prison were of great significance for the development of the theology and future of the church.

In 1953, the SCM Press published a collection of these letters and some poems in translation under the heading *Letters and Papers from Prison*. Priscilla Collins, wife of William Collins of the publishing firm, who was responsible for Fontana Paperbacks and the religious output, heard a broadcast and was struck by the relevance of the poems. She made enquiries and discovered that there were collected volumes of Bonhoeffer's writings being published in Germany. She asked me to translate them. By then, I had already reviewed the first volume of these collected writings for *The Bridge* (the journal of the German British Christian Fellowship). They were collected by Eberhard Bethge and eventually arranged in five volumes, covering Bonhoeffer's addresses at ecumenical gatherings, his essays, and his letters, all arranged according to subject matter, with one volume of sermons. It did not seem wise to translate all of this material, but I arranged it in chronological order and published the translation, much of it by John Bowden, in three volumes: "No Rusty Swords," "The Way to Freedom," and "True Patriotism." A separate booklet was published of his lectures on "Christology."

While we were engaged in this work, Eberhard Bethge published his biography of Dietrich Bonhoeffer, a mammoth work of nearly a thousand pages. Priscilla Collins asked if I would translate this into English. This meant working through the biography with Eberhard Bethge and his wife, Renate. We edited it down a little and I supervised a team of translators so that it was published in English in 1970.

In the midst of all this activity with Bonhoeffer's writings, many attempts were made to portray this exceptional man on radio, TV, film, and stage. Vernon Sproxton and Wilfred Harrison were most assiduous in this and kept in touch with me. Eventually I decided that we needed a radio program which would bring out the heart of his thinking. I settled for a formula which had proved successful with other thinkers—"The Imaginary Conversation." This was a reconstruction of a conversation which could have happened. I chose two: the first with Teilhard de Chardin in London in the thirties; the second with Richard Niebuhr in New York the night before Bonhoeffer decided to return to Germany. The producer of these programs was Terence Tiller, who one day asked if there was a short work he could read to let him know this man Bonhoeffer better. I wrote a brief biography for him which was published in 1966 by Lutterworth Press.

There had been so many approaches to Bonhoeffer through his poems, his letters, his books, and his life, that I felt the need eventually to write a biography—not to compete with Eberhard Bethge—no one could do that—but to make available something more accessible. It was published by Hodder & Stoughton in 1987 as *The Shame and the Sacrifice*. Two years later, I followed that with *The Legacy of Dietrich Bonhoeffer* which attempted to produce the book Bonhoeffer himself wanted to write, but did not live to do more than the summary. Bonhoeffer was again on my study table when I wrote a book on George Bell, published in 1995 by the Council of Churches for Britain and Ireland and entitled *Unshakeable Friend*. That year was a busy time for all who knew anything about Bonhoeffer and I found myself lecturing in many places. It was then I saw that the real heart of Bonhoeffer's thinking lies in his poetry and that, beautiful as the existing translations were, a new translation of them all was needed. This new collection includes the whole of the "Death of Moses" for the first time in English.

INTRODUCTION

Dietrich Bonhoeffer was born in Breslau on February 4, 1906, into a German family of good standing. His father was a distinguished neurologist, who, when Dietrich was six, was appointed to a senior post in the University of Berlin as director of a clinic for mental disorders. He was the senior psychiatrist in Germany at the time. Dietrich's forebears included mayors and scientists on his father's side and on his mother's side he was the great-grandson of Karl von Hase, Professor of Church History in Jena.

Although born in Breslau, now part of Poland, Berlin was his hometown for most of his life. There he grew up in a fashionable part of the city, with neighbors from the various faculties of the university. These early days were pleasant and comfortable despite the deprivations of the First World War and the years that followed it.

The Bonhoeffers were Lutherans, but not inordinately religious. The so-called Prussian mandates were their guide, but not in a restricting way: they called for loyalty to church and state, devotion to family, and commitment to the Protestant ethical imperative.

Dietrich alone of the eight children chose to study theology. He was educated at Tübingen and Berlin. After a period of pastoral duties in a German-speaking congregation in Barcelona, he spent a year as a Sloane Student at Union Theological Seminary, New York. He was influenced by Karl Barth, but was only a visiting student at his lectures in Bonn. Dietrich was licensed as a lecturer in the University of Berlin at an early age, his academic theses were commended by such as Barth, and for a time he served a local church in Berlin. He was a promising theologian and an influential pastor. He had a successful career ahead of him.

Even before Hitler came to power, the Bonhoeffer family were strongly opposed to National Socialism and they had no sympathy for communism, apparently the only alternative at that time.

Dietrich was much concerned with the effect of Nazi teaching upon the churches. He was soon involved in what was called the "Church Struggle," which divided many of the churches in Germany, especially the Church of the Old Prussian Union to which the Bonhoeffers belonged and of which Dietrich was an ordained minister. The struggle was between those who saw Hitler as the savior of Germany in its destiny to establish a German Protestantism, the German Christians, and those who saw the dangers of National Socialism and sought to defend the churches from it, the Confessing Church.

Bonhoeffer was at once on the side of the Confessing Church, although he criticized it for not going far enough. He called for a protest against the treatment of

Jews and could not get the Confessing Church to support this protest. He did, however, bring the Ecumenical Movement, headed by Bishop Bell of Chichester, to
throw its weight behind the Confessing Church and
condemn the German Christians.

For two years, 1933 to 1935, Bonhoeffer served as
minister to two German-speaking congregations in London and made the close acquaintance of Bishop Bell. He
and the bishop worked ardently to acquaint the world
Church with what was going on in Germany. Bonhoeffer supplied Bell with accurate information and the
bishop spoke out in protest as a member of the House of
Lords and with the authority of the Ecumenical Movement. These two years were critical for Bonhoeffer and
for the Church Struggle. In 1935, he returned to Germany to start a theological seminary of the Confessing
Church, eventually situated at Finkenwalde in Pomerania. As director of that seminary he met Eberhard
Bethge, a senior student who later became his colleague
and close friend. The seminary was closed by the author-
ities in 1937 and Bonhoeffer continued clandestine studies with his students in various parts of Pomerania and
by correspondence.

In 1939, when his year was called up for military service, he had serious problems. He was a loyal German,
but was unable to take an oath of loyalty to Adolf Hitler,
which was required at that time. He consulted with the
Bishop of Chichester and other international friends.

Reinhold Niebuhr arranged for an invitation to America with a series of lectures planned. He accepted and went to New York only to dicover that his friends were trying to rescue him from Nazi Germany. When the war clouds gathered he cancelled his lecture tours and returned to Germany.

Back home he was invited by his brother-in-law, Hans von Dohnanyi, to join a group conspiring to overthrow the Nazi Government and place Hitler on trial for crimes which von Dohnanyi carefully listed. The political resistance group was the *Abwehr* (military intelligence, a kind of M15). For years the secret conspiracy was safe because the Gestapo were not able to investigate the *Abwehr.* Bonhoeffer was appointed to the *Abwehr* and travelled on a Nazi passport during the war to neutral countries. His official role was to bring the churches of these countries on to the German side. He did the opposite: one of his missions was to take a party of Jews to Switzerland. He was frequently in Denmark and Norway after they were occupied. In 1942, at Whitsuntide, he met Bishop Bell in Sweden and gave him plans for a coup which was to overthrow the Nazi Government. All the conspirators asked of Britain was that they would deal honorably with a non-Nazi government and not impose conditions of humiliation on Germany. Memories of Versailles were very bitter and Bonhoeffer shared them. Bishop Bell did his best to persuade the British government of the likely success of this coup, but

Anthony Eden would give no such assurances. The military in Germany withdrew much of their support and those who remained in the conspiracy saw no other way than assassination. Many attempts were made of which Bonhoeffer approved. By the time of the final and fatal failure of July 20, 1944, Bonhoeffer was in prison. He had been arrested on April 5, 1943. On April 29, he was charged with "subversion of the armed forces," which meant that he was discouraging his students from military service. He was imprisoned for two years. For the greater part of that time he was held in one of the military interrogation prisons in Tegel, a suburb of Berlin which he knew well. It was there that he wrote most of his letters to Eberhard Bethge, his parents, and his fiancée, Maria von Wedemeyer, as well as the outline of a book which he hoped to write on the future of his church and nine of his ten poems. He was able to obtain writing paper, books, and other means of communication with the outside world. He wrote a number of things about Germany and even attempted a novel as well as a drama. On October 8, 1944, all this changed when he was transferred to a detention cellar in Prinz Albrecht Strasse, the house prison of the Reich Security Head Office. Later he was moved from one venue to another as the Allied forces advanced from the west and the Russians from the east. He was for a while at Buchenwald and twice at Flossenburg, where he was executed on April 9, 1945, within sound of American guns.

During his two years in prison his mood changed and his knowledge both of his church and of himself grew. He was kept informed of events taking place outside and these influenced his thinking, as did the many books he was able to read—not the least of which was the Bible as he followed the Christian Year and kept its festivals in prison.

The importance of the poems he wrote lies in the fact that they were the ultimate attempt to express his deepest feelings about himself, his friends, his church, the future of Germany, and his own future. The last poem he wrote recalled all the wonderful privileges he had had and faced the twin possibilities—death or a future in freedom. It is the last poem in this book: "By Kindly Powers Surrounded." He wrote it in the detention cellar in Prinz Albrecht Strasse.

At first Bonhoeffer kept his poems to himself, but early in June 1944, he sent his first poem to Eberhard Bethge and shortly afterwards to Maria. It asked whether all the beauty of the past was gone forever.

VERGANGENHEIT

———

Loss!

Vergangenheit—Loss!

You walk away—love's happiness and sore pain.
What name shall I give you? Distress, life, bliss,
part of myself, my heart—times past? All gone?
The door slams shut,
I hear your footsteps slowly die away.
What is left when you are gone? Joy, anguish,
        longing?
I know only this: you go away—and all is gone.

Can you feel now, how I clutch at you,
how I hold you so tight
that it must hurt you?
How I open the wounds,
that your blood may flow,
only to be sure that you keep close to me,
you, so full of real and earthly life?
Can you sense that I have now a terrible longing
for my own suffering?
That I yearn to see my own blood flow,
only that all may not sink
into times that are gone?

Life, what have you done to me?
Why did you come? Why do you pass away?
Times past, if you flee from me,
are you not still my past, mine?

As the sun sets ever more quickly over the ocean,
sucked into the darkness,
so sinks and sinks and sinks,
relentlessly,
your image into the sea of forgetfulness,
engulfed in a few waves.
As a puff of warm breath
dissolves in the cool air of morning,
so fades your image,
until your face, your hands, your figure
I no longer know.
A laugh, a glance, a gesture appears to me,
then it fades,
disappears,
without comfort, without your nearness,
it is destroyed,
an illusion from the past.

I want to breathe the air of your being,
absorb it, lose myself in it,
as on a hot summer's day, the heavy blossom
invites the bees,
and intoxicates them;
as the mohawk becomes drunk from the privet;
but a rough wind destroys the fragrance and the
      blossom,
and I stand like a fool,
as all vanishes and is gone.

To me, it is as though red-hot pincers
tear pieces from my flesh,
when you, my past life, rush away from me.
Mad defiance and raging anger seize me,
I fling wild and meaningless questions into the air.
Why and why and why? Always the same question.
If my senses cannot hold you,
my vanishing passing life,
I will think and think again
until I find what I have lost.

But something tells me
that all around me, within and without,
laughs at me, unmoved and puzzled
by my useless labors,
snaring the wind,
to win back what is past and gone.

Eye and soul become evil,
I hate what I see,
I hate what moves me,
I hate all that is alive and beautiful,
all that should console me for my loss.
I want my life, I demand my own life back,
my past life,
You!

You! Tears fill my eyes;
perhaps through the veil of tears
I will win you back,
the total vision,
the whole of you.
No! I will not weep.
Only the strong are helped by tears,
the weak are made weaker.

I am tired as evening comes,
welcome is my cell,
which promises forgetfulness
when possession is denied me.
Night, quench the fire that burns,
send to me full forgetfulness,
be kind to me, night, and perform your gentle art,
to you I entrust myself.
But the night is strong and wise,
stronger than the day and wiser than me.
What no earthly power can do,
where thinking and feeling, defiance and tears must
    fail,
the night showers its full riches upon me.
Undefiled by hostile time,
pure, free and whole,
the dream brings you to me,
you, from the past, you, my life,
you, from past days and past hours.

By your presence, I am awakened in deepest night,
and cry out—
are you again lost to me? do I seek you ever in vain,
my beloved of past days?
I stretch out my hands
and pray—
and I learn something new:

> That which is past will return to you again
> as your life's most living strain,
> through thanks and through repentance.
> Lay hold on God's forgiveness in the past,
> pray that he will care for you this day and to the
>   last.

COMMENTARY ON
"Vergangenheit"

The first problem with this poem is its title. When Eberhard Bethge received a copy, he made his usual frank comments and then added: "I wonder if you ought to find a more propitious title." Bonhoeffer had told him that he was gong to send it to his fiancée, but Bethge felt that it sounded pretty final, as though the whole love affair was over—*Vergangenheit* means past and gone.

It was, however, not only his love for Maria that gave substance to this poem; it was his deep concern about the possible separation from his own past—had he lost it? What kind of a person had he become? And was that person still the one of former times?

In the English version, I have therefore chosen simply "Loss" as a title. The process of examining what had happened to his church and those who, like him, had resisted the evils of Nazism, began well before he was arrested. A letter sent to some of his friends at the end of 1942 shows that he had already given careful thought to what they had lost and whether they were of any use for the rebuilding of the church and nation once the war ended. Part of that circular letter reads:

> We have been silent witnesses of evil deeds; we have been drenched by many storms; we have learned the art of equivocation and pretence; experience has

made us suspicious of others and kept us from being truthful and open; intolerable conflicts have worn us down and even made us cynical. Are we still of any use? (LPP, 16)

The starting point of this poem was a visit from Maria and it was addressed primarily to her. He was aware that he was not the same person as he had been at her age. In a letter written to her after some disagreements he expresses this:

Listen, Maria, I want to tell you something. I'm much older than you. I too have known that insensate, heady, uncertain desire in my time. It was never fulfilled. I was once in love with a girl; she became a theologian; and our paths ran parallel for many years. She was about my age. I was twenty-one when it began. We didn't realize we loved each other. More than eight years went by. Then we discovered the truth from a third person who thought he was helping us. We then discussed the matter frankly but it was too late. We had evaded and misunderstood each other for too long. We could never be entirely in sympathy again, and I told her so. (LLC 92, 208)

He added that later, when he heard of her marriage to someone else, "the weight on my mind gradually lessened."

Working on this poem, I am not quite convinced that he no longer felt that "insensate, heady, uncertain desire" for Maria.

That letter to Maria was May 19, 1944. A week later he sent the poem, first to Eberhard Bethge and a little later to Maria. To Eberhard, he made a comment:

> This dialogue with the past, the attempt to hold on to it and above all the fear of losing it, is the almost daily accompaniment of my life here [in prison]; and sometimes, especially after brief visits which are always followed by long partings, it becomes a theme with variations. (LPP, 319)

"Vergangenheit" or "Loss" is a love poem and is directly linked to an emotional moment after a brief visit from Maria, but Bonhoeffer feared that Maria might understand it as only that. He therefore directs her attention to the rhyming lines at the end, from which he says it all began. She is expected to find comfort in those rhymes which she could easily memorize. Bethge, however, points out that she cannot be expected to read the poem objectively. It is about the total changes from the past and the need to make use of those past experiences, however painful they may be. The poem is carefully structured in blank verse—except for the final five lines in rhyme.

It begins with the occasion—the visit, the closing door, the retreating steps, the silence.

The immediate reaction is strongly worded—confused, longing, passionate desire—leading to the lover's longing to suffer.

This context next provides him with symbols for his dialogue with the past—the sun sinking over the horizon, the visible breath on a cold morning evaporating, the bees on a hot summer day blown away by the rough wind. All three of these images depict graphically what he has already cried out, "Life, what have you done to me?" and the Job-like protest, "Why did you come? Why do you pass away?" followed by his central question which is repeated later in many ways:

> Times past, if you flee from me,
> are you not still my past, mine?

It is that question that stands behind the three colorful examples of the sun, the breath, and the bees. He grows in conviction that the examples are not exact parallels and explores the possibility of the past being still there for him to draw upon.

In the separation from Maria and also from Eberhard he feels the pain of loss. There follows a powerful expression of frustration, flinging meaningless questions into the air, "Why and why and why? Always the same question."

He demands his past life, as though it had been stolen from him. The sorrow almost breaks him and he seeks solace in sleep. Bonhoeffer attaches great importance to the symbols of light and dark in other poems. Here is a twofold use of night:

> Night, quench the fire that burns,
> Send to me full forgetfulness,
> be kind to me, night, and perform your gentle art,
> to you I entrust myself.

Then he praises the night as wise and strong, doing "what no earthly power can do." The role of the dream is well expressed.

With the awakening comes loss and he cries out and prays. Then, the flash comes, an experience of something new. What God has done in the past he can do again. Maria, remember that!

> That which is past will return to you again.

Remembering the past "through thanks and through repentance" leads to a confidence in the future. This is no facile optimism, but the essence of Christian hope.

GLÜCK UND UNGLÜCK

———

Success and Failure

GLÜCK UND UNGLÜCK—*SUCCESS AND FAILURE*

Success and failure
suddenly strike and overpower us,
both the same at first,
like the touch of burning heat and freezing cold,
indistinguishable.
Like meteors
flung from distant heavens,
blazing and threatening,
over our heads.
Those visited stand bemused
amidst the ruins
of their dull, daily lives.

Proud and exalted,
destroying, subduing,
success and failure,
invited or uninvited,
hold festival with
these shattered people.
Dressed and decorated,
the visited
prepare for the sacrificial feast.

Success is full of foreboding,
failure has its sweetness.
Without distinction they appear to come,

the one or the other,
from the unknown.
Both are proud and terrible.
People come from far and wide,
walk by and look,
pausing to stare,
half envious, half afraid,
at the outrage,
where the supernatural,
blessing and cursing at the same time,
entangling and disentangling,
sets forth the drama of human life.
What is success and what is failure?

Time alone distinguishes.
When the incomprehensible, exciting,
sudden event
lapses into wearisome waiting,
when the creeping hours of the day
first reveal the true outlines of failure,
then most give up,
weary of the monotony
of oft-repeated failure,
disappointed and bored with themselves.

That is the hour of steadfast love,
the hour of the mother and the beloved,
the hour of the friend and the brother.

Steadfast love transforms all failure,
and gently cradles it
in the soft
radiance of heavenly light.

COMMENTARY ON
"Glück und Unglück"

This time there are no problems about the title in German, which is also the first line of the poem and the issue dealt with throughout. But there is a problem of translation. The juxtaposition of these two words occupied much of Bonhoeffer's thinking during May 1944. In that month, Dietrich Wilhelm Rüdiger Bethge was born, baptized, and his father had home leave. Eberhard's relationship to Renate, his wife, had certain parallels with Bonhoeffer's to Maria. Eberhard was not in prison, but he was separated by military service on the Italian front. Like Maria, Renate was very young, much younger than Eberhard. During this time of home leave, Bonhoeffer drafted comments on the *"Losungen"* (meditation texts that were much in use for daily prayer at that time). It was Whitsuntide. Bonhoeffer continued to send these comments until Eberhard left for his unit on June 8. The text for May 30 was Genesis 39:23: "The LORD was with Joseph and whatever he did, *The LORD made it prosper.*" Luther's translation of that last phrase is, *"dazu gab der Herr Glück."* William Tyndale has the lively and attractive translation, "and Joseph was a lucky fellow." Our word "luck" comes from the same root as *"Glück."* Bonhoeffer commented upon the *Glück* of married life, which he was denied by imprisonment and which Eberhard found disturbed by military service. In the sermon which Bonhoeffer sent for the baptism of the young child, he comments upon the good fortune of being brought up in a stable home, where both parents had had stable homes themselves. "You are lucky," he says, using the word *"glücklich."* Bonhoeffer shows a wide use of these words, *"Glück"* and *"Unglück."* In the novel that he was attempting to write a little earlier he has a scene in which a kindly major tries to warn an eager Nazi lieutenant against the harshness of his views:

> But Christoph, dear Christoph, if you want to be hard, do not glory in your hardness. If you want to be inexorable in order to have your own way do not forget to excuse yourself and to give way whenever it is possible. If you must despise life to gain it, don't forget to love it when you have gained it. Above all, beware of speaking lightly of happiness [*Glück*] or flirting with unhappiness [*Unglück*]. (*True Patriotism*, Collins, 1973, 233)

How shall we, then, translate the title and first line? "Joy and Sorrow," "Good and Evil," "Happiness and Unhappiness," "Lucky and Unlucky," "Fortune and Misfortune," or even "Blessing and Curse"?

Bonhoeffer was reading the poems of Hölderlin, whose long poem "Patmos," seems to have affected him as he wrote his Whitsun message to Maria:

> God is near
> and hard to grasp,
> but where danger is,
> the caring hand appears. (Hölderlin)

His Whitsun message to Maria was:

> He that is blest is himself a blessing. Let us wish that
> for each other and be that to all those for whom we
> work and for whom we care. That someone should
> be a blessing to others is the greatest thing of all isn't
> it? Not just a helpmate, or a companion or a friend,
> but a blessing. (LLC 92, 203)

The final stanza of the poem needs this comment.

But far more than his reading or his correspondence
with either Maria or Eberhard were the events going on
outside his prison walls—the "Conspiracy." Only two
years before, also at Whitsun (1942), he had met with the
Bishop of Chichester and laid before him plans for the
overthrow of the Nazi Regime and the end of the war.
That had failed. Other assassination attempts had also
failed. Now, within a few weeks, an attempt was to be
made upon Hitler's life which had every prospect of success. If it succeeded, what kind of regime would replace
Hitler's Reich? Success could be turned into the worst
kind of failure. If it failed and all the conspirators were
discovered, something even more terrible was possible—
as time revealed. His anxieties at this time have therefore
led me to translate the title: "Success and Failure."

The poem recognizes that while success and failure are opposites, they can be almost indistinguishable. It points out the arbitrariness of the two and how they are outside our control. Either can take hold of us and destroy us. When at last you know that what looked like success has been revealed in its true outlines as failure, then only steadfast love can help transform that failure into success. The poem keeps us pondering the inexplicable nature of *Glück* and *Unglück*—fortune and misfortune, joy and sorrow, happiness and unhappiness, building up and tearing down, luckiness and unluckiness, good and evil, success and failure—all are enigmatic.

WER BIN ICH?

Who Am I?

Wer bin Ich?—*Who Am I?*

Who am I? They often tell me,
I step out from my cell,
composed, contented and sure,
like a lord from his manor.

Who am I? They often tell me,
I speak with my jailers,
frankly, familiar and firm,
as though I was in command.

Who am I? They also tell me,
I bear the days of hardship,
unconcerned, amused and proud,
like one who usually wins.

Am I really what others tell me?
Or am I only what I myself know of me?
Troubled, homesick, ill, like a bird in a cage,
gasping for breath, as though one strangled me,
hungering for colors, for flowers, for songs of birds,
thirsting for kind words, for human company,
quivering with anger at despotism and petty insults,
anxiously waiting for great events,
helplessly worrying about friends far away,
empty and tired of praying, of thinking, of working,
exhausted and ready to bid farewell to it all.

Who am I? This or the other?
Am I then, this today and the other tomorrow?
Am I both at the same time? In public, a hypocrite
and by myself, a contemptible, whining weakling?
Or am I to myself, like a beaten army,
flying in disorder from a victory already won?

Who am I? Lonely questions mock me.
Who I really am, you know me, I am thine, O God!

COMMENTARY ON
"Wer bin Ich?"

There is no problem with the title—"Who Am I?"—which again is the first line of the poem, carefully structured and balanced throughout. Even how it appears on the page is designed. The short lines in the first section, which deals with the opinions others have of him, contrast with the longer lines of his own self-analysis.

The slightest tendency towards introspection is nurtured within the enclosed atmosphere of a prison cell—a bed, a shelf, a stool, a bucket—within a confined space, locked away from the outside world. In addition, a spyhole reminds the prisoner that he can be seen at any time without knowing who is looking. To be always under possible observation, without being able to look back, leads inevitably to the questions:

> "What do they see from outside?"
> "What do I see of that same person from within?"
> "Do both see the same person?"

Writing to Bethge, on December 15, 1943, about eight months after his arrest, Bonhoeffer says:

> When I read your letter yesterday, I felt as though a spring had begun again to produce the first few drops of water after a long time, in which as a result my intellectual life was beginning to dry up. (LPP, 160)

He admitted that he had been forced to live in the past, rather than the future "which lies more in the realm of hope than in the realm of possession and tangible experience." Eberhard's letter had set his thoughts working "after they had grown rusty and tired during recent weeks." He begins to recall the past in a less gloomy mood, and as the electricity fails, he writes by candlelight:

> So I imagine the two of us sitting together as we used to in the old days after supper, in my room upstairs, smoking, occasionally strumming chords on the clavichord, and discussing the day's events. (LPP, 161)

Having recreated that encounter, he comes to his greatest concern:

> I often wonder who I really am—the man who goes on squirming under these ghastly experiences and in wretchedness cries to heaven, or the man who scourges himself and pretends to others (and even to himself) that he is placid, cheerful, composed and in control of himself, and allows people to admire him for it (i.e. for playing a part—or is it *not* playing a part?). What does one's attitude mean anyway? In short, I know less than ever about myself, and I'm no longer attaching any importance to it. I've had more than enough psychology, and I'm less inclined to analyze the state of my soul. (LPP, 162)

He passes on to other things, but this is an early indication that the substance of this poem is already forming in his mind.

Much later, in his very important theological letter of July 8, 1944, he counters the view that a person's essential nature consists of his "inner life," which is thought of as "those secret human places" where God is (supposed) to have his domain. Against this he asserts a biblical position:

> The Bible does not recognize our distinction between the outward and the inward. Why should it? It is always concerned with the whole person, even where, as in the Sermon on the Mount, the Decalogue is pressed home to refer to an inward disposition. That a good disposition can take the place of total goodness is quite unbiblical. (LPP, 346)

He had already started to send poems to Eberhard, and now he sends "Who Am I?" which repeats ideas already found in the letters. And, despite his earlier rejection of psychology, this poem is a kind of self-analysis.

CHRISTEN UND HEIDEN

———

Christians and Others

CHRISTEN UND HEIDEN—*CHRISTIANS AND OTHERS*

1. All go to God in their distress,
seek help and pray for bread and happiness,
deliverance from pain, guilt and death.
All do, Christians and others.

2. All go to God in His distress,
find him poor, reviled without shelter or bread,
watch him tormented by sin, weakness, and death.
Christians stand by God in His agony.

3. God goes to all in their distress,
satisfies body and soul with His bread,
dies, crucified for all, Christians and others
and both alike forgiving.

COMMENTARY ON
"Christen und Heiden"

The most obvious translation of the title and its echo throughout the poem is "Christians and Pagans," but that emphasizes the contrast, while the poem leads to common forgiveness. The difference is there only in the line, "Christians stand by God in His agony." I have tried to avoid the harshness of "pagans," which is much harsher in English use than is the German *"Heiden."* The Jews, for example, used *Heiden* to mean Gentiles and it was not derogatory. For this reason, I have taken the liberty to translate the title "Christians and Others."

With a background of the common bond, which can be seen in the first stanza as "need" and in the last stanza as "forgiveness," the last line of the middle stanza stands out as the crucial line. This brings to mind the picture of Mary, the mother of Jesus, and John, "the disciple whom Jesus loved," standing at the foot of the cross, where Jesus pleads for forgiveness for his persecutors—"they know not what they do." Mary and John stand by the cross— "God in His agony."

After writing this poem, Bonhoeffer said in a letter of July 16:

> It is not the religious act that makes the Christian, but the participation in the suffering of God in the world. (LPP, 361)

Any translator would have difficulty with the metrical and rhyming form in this poem, as indeed Bonhoeffer himself did. The original is scored with innumerable changes. The rhyming pattern is not only within each stanza, but even between the stanzas. The first English translation bravely attempted this tight hymn-like structure. I think the content of the poem suffered from this and have therefore not tried to follow the form exactly, falling back on Bonhoeffer's words, "It's not the rhyme that makes the poem, but the poem that makes the rhyme."

Is this poem then "universalist"—are Christians and others alike at the end? Where is the privilege of the believer? By now, Bonhoeffer had observed Christians and others, finding, as he said, that it was easier to talk about God with unbelievers than with Christians.

One is reminded of the answer given by Jürgen Moltmann to the question, "Are you, then, a universalist?" to which as a good Calvinist he had to say "No!" but added, "I sometimes suspect that God is."

NÄCHTLICHE STIMMEN

—

Voices in the Night

NÄCHTLICHE STIMMEN—*VOICES IN THE NIGHT*

Stretched out upon my prison bed,
I stare at the empty wall.
Outside, a summer evening,
regardless of me,
goes singing into the country.
Softly ebbs the tide of the day
on the eternal shore.
Sleep awhile!
Refresh body and soul, head and hand!
Outside, people, houses; hearts and spirits are aflame.
Until the blood-red night
dawns upon your day—
hold your ground!

In the stillness of the night,
I listen.
Only footsteps and shouts of the guards,
a loving couple in the distance, stifled laughter.
Can you hear nothing else, you sluggish sleeper?
I hear my own soul totter and tremble.
Nothing else?
I hear, I hear,
like voices, like shouts,
like cries for help,
the waking dreams of fellow-sufferers,
dumb thoughts in the night.

I hear the restless creaking of the beds,
I hear chains.
I hear men toss and turn in sleeplessness,
longing for freedom and vengeful action.
When sleep overcomes them in the morning hours,
they murmur in their dreams of wife and children.
I hear the lisping pleasure of half-grown boys,
enjoying their childish dreams.
I hear them pull up their blankets
and hide themselves from the horrible nightmares.
I hear the sighs and light breathing of the old,
who prepare themselves quietly for the great
      journey.
They have seen right and wrong come and go,
now they wish to see the imperishable and eternal.

Night and silence.
Only footsteps and shouts of the guards.
Do you not hear it in this silenced house,
shaking, breaking and collapsing,
as hundreds kindle the glowing ember of their
      hearts?

    Their songs they hide,
my ears are open wide.
"We who are old, and we who are young,
we children of every tongue,
we who are strong, and we who find it hard,

we who sleep, and we who guard,
we who are poor, and we who have all,
together into failure fall,
we who are good and we who are unclean,
whatever we have been,
we men with scars we cannot hide,
we witnesses of those who died,
we who are defiant and we who are bemused,
we who are innocent and we who are accused,
by long isolation, sorely abused.
Brother, we seek and call for thee!
Brother do you hear me?"

Twelve cold, thin strokes of the tower clock
awaken me.
There is in them no music, no warmth,
to shelter and comfort me.
Angry, barking dogs at midnight
startle me,
cold, joyless strokes,
divide a poor yesterday
from a poor today.
Can one day change to another,
finding nothing new, nothing better,
and in a short time end like this—
what can it mean to me?

I will see the times change,
when signs light up the heavens,
new bells ring over the people,
growing louder and louder.

I wait for that midnight,
in which the shining splendor
dazzles and destroys the evil in our fear,
to establish with joy that which is right.

Evil concealed
is revealed
at the bar.

Betrayal and tricks,
intolerable conflicts,
will find atonement soon.

Let people confess,
the power of goodness
works righteousness.

Rejoice and declare:
justice and care
to a new generation.

Heaven, give birth
to peace and worth
for the sons of earth.

Earth will see,
people, become free,
be free!

Suddenly, I wake up,
as though, from a sinking ship, I sighted land,
as though there was something firm to grasp,
as though fruit was ripening to gold.
But when I look, grasp or hold,
there is only an impenetrable mass of darkness.

I sink into brooding,
I lower myself into the heart of darkness.
You, night, full of horror and evil,
make yourself known to me!
Why and how long will you gnaw at our patience?
Silence, deep and long,
then I hear the night, as it comes down to me:
"I am not dark, the darkness is your guilt!"

Guilt! I hear a trembling and a shudder,
a murmur and a cry,
I hear men in angry mood.
Innumerable voices in wild confusion,
a dumb choir
assaults the ear of God.

   "Hunted by men and maligned,
    defenseless and guilty to their mind,

by intolerable burdens abused,
yet we declare them the accused.

'e accuse those who drove us to the evil deed,
who allowed us to share their guilty seed,
who made us witnesses of the just abused,
only to despise those they had used.

Our eyes must see violence,
entangling us in their guilty offense;
Then as they silence our voice,
like dumb dogs we have no choice.

We learned to call lies just
uniting ourselves with the unjust.
When violence was done to the weak,
our cold eyes did not speak.

And what in sorrow our hearts had broken,
remained hidden and unspoken.
We quenched our burning ire
and stamped out the inner fire.

Sacred bonds by which we once were bound
are now torn and fallen to the ground,
friendship and truth betrayed,
tears and remorse in ridicule displayed.

We sons from upright men descended,
who once rights and truth defended,
have now become despisers of God and man,
amidst the mocking laughter of hell's plan."

Though robbed of freedom and honor,
we stand tall before men with pride.
And when we are wrongly decried,
before men we declare our innocence freely.

At peace and firm, we stand man to man,
and accuse those who accuse us.

Only before Thee, maker of all,
before Thee alone are we sinners.

Shrinking from pain and poor in deeds,
we have betrayed Thee before men.

Though we saw lies raise their head,
we dishonored the truth instead.

We saw brothers dying while we had breath
and feared only our own death.

We come before Thee as men,
confessing our sins.

Lord, after the ferment of these days,
send us times to prove us.
After so much wrong,
let us see the day dawn!

As far as the eye can see,
let thy word provide ways for us.

Until you have washed away our guilt
hold us in quiet patience.

We will prepare ourselves in quietness
until you call us to new times.
Until you still the storm and abate the flood,
and your will works wonders.

Brothers, until the night is passed,
pray for me!

The first light of morning steals through my
        window,
pale and bleak.
A light wind brushes my brow
with the warmth of summer.
"A summer's day," all I can say is, "lovely summer's
        day."
What might it bring to me?
Outside I hear hurried, hesitant steps go by.
They suddenly stop by me.

I go hot and cold,
I know, oh, I know!
Hold fast, brother, soon it will be all over,
soon, soon.
I hear you march with brave and proud steps.
This moment you see no longer,
your eyes are on future times.
I go with you, brother, to that place,
and I hear your last word:
"Brother, when the sun shines no longer for me,
you must live for me!"

Stretched out upon my prison bed,
I stare at the empty wall.
Outside a summer morning,
regardless of me,
goes rejoicing into the country.
Brother, while the long night waits,
until our day dawns,
we shall hold our ground!

COMMENTARY ON
"Nächtliche Stimmen"

With his letter to Eberhard Bethge of July 8 and 9, Bonhoeffer enclosed the two short poems *"Wer bin Ich?"* and *"Christen und Heiden."* Of *"Nächtliche Stimmen,"* described as "about this place," he says he would much rather talk with him about it, and show it to him. There is no doubt that although he thought it was not too bad and that "one day it will get out," he was anxious about "Voices in the Night." His anxiety stemmed both from fears that the poem might fall into the wrong hands and because Bethge was partly responsible for this poem. He had suggested that someone should give Bonhoeffer a copy of Dostoyevsky's *Memoirs from the House of the Dead.* Bonhoeffer had read it earlier, but when he now received a copy it came much nearer to his own experience and its influence on this poem is obvious.

On July 25, having already written this poem, he comments on *Memoirs from the House of the Dead,* which he had just finished reading again. He writes that he is still thinking about the assertion that "man cannot live without hope, and that men who have really lost all hope often become wild and wicked." The failure of the July Plot is now known to him and he is even more anxious about the poem. Two days later he writes to Bethge again, asking, "Have you got the poems—all three?"

The reading of Dostoyevsky led him to think of those outside the prison as indifferent to those in prison. On July 16, before the failure, Bonhoeffer writes concerning the non-moral sympahy Dostoyevsky talks of: "May not this amorality, the product of religiosity, be an essential trait of these people, and also help us to understand more recent events" (LPP, 358).

The poem begins with that thought—the contrast between those suffering in prison because they have seen the "reality" of what is happening and those "outside" who are unaware of the "unreality" of their own lives. The poem is strained—it has a difficult rhyme and rhythm. In translation, I have only retained that form when it seemed to be necessary to create the atmosphere of the poem. Usually these are short lines. For example, when after describing the suffering of those in prison, he bursts out with the short, sporadic lines:

> Evil concealed
> is revealed
> at the bar.

An important part of this poem is Bonhoeffer's assertion that even those who, like him, resisted the "monstrous tyranny" were guilty. But he will not accept this guilt before men.

Though robbed of freedom and honor,
we stand tall before men with pride.

Before God, the guilt must be admitted:

At peace and firm, we stand man to man;
and accuse those who accuse us.

Only before Thee, maker of all,
before Thee alone are we sinners.

After the darkest passage in the poem, his hope rises, a Christian hope which is based upon firm foundations:

Lord, after the ferment of these days,
send us times to prove us.
After so much wrong,
let us see the day dawn!

For these new times, he declares, "We will prepare ourselves in quietness." One is reminded of his sermon for the baptism of Dietrich Rüdiger Bethge, when he reflected that "Till then, the Christian cause will be a silent and hidden affair, but there will be those who pray and do right and wait for God's own time" (LPP, 300).

The poem ends as the morning light comes through the small window high up in his cell, and a prisoner goes out to execution.

He was not unaware that this might well be his own
end—as it was—and his last lines are now his last word
to those of us who live:

Brother, when the sun shines no longer for me,
you must live for me!

STATIONEN AUF DEM WEGE ZUR FREIHEIT

———

Stages on the Way to Freedom

STATIONEN AUF DEM WEGE ZUR FREIHEIT—
STAGES ON THE WAY TO FREEDOM

Discipline

If you are drawn to seek freedom, learn first of all
to discipline yourself and your senses, lest desires
and your members lead you hither and thither.
Pure and chaste be your body and spirit, totally
    under control,
and obedient, seeking the goal which is set for them.
No one experiences the secret of freedom, except
    by discipline.

Action

Choose and do what is right, not what fancy takes,
not weighing the possibilities, but bravely grasping
    the real,
not in the flight of ideas, but only in action is there
    freedom.
Come away from your anxious hesitations into the
    storm of events,
carried by God's command and your faith alone.
Then freedom will embrace your spirit with rejoicing.

Suffering

Wondrous is the change. The strong active hands
are bound now. Powerless and alone, you see the end

of your action. Yet, you breathe a sigh of relief and
    lay it aside
quietly trusting to stronger hands and are content.
Only for a moment did you touch the bliss of
    freedom,
then you gave it back to God that he might
    gloriously fulfill it.

Death

Come now, highest feast on the way to everlasting
    freedom,
death. Lay waste the burdens of chains and walls
which confine our earthly bodies and blinded souls,
that we see at last what here we could not see.
Freedom, we sought you long in discipline, action
    and suffering.
Dying, we recognize you now in the face of God.

COMMENTARY ON
"Stationen auf dem Wege zur Freiheit"

The word *"Stationen"* is correctly translated as "stages" or even "steps," but this is a meditation poem and it recalls John 14:2, "In my Father's house are many *mansions*." The old rendering recalls the Latin, *mansio,* which is a stopping place on a journey. It is that idea which is contained in this meditation on "freedom." Bonhoeffer's sense of *Stationen* is of "lodging places on the way."

This poem was composed after the failed attempt on the life of Hitler (July 20, 1944). Bonhoeffer was working in the sick bay of his prison when he heard the news of the attempted assassination on the radio. Over the following weeks the Gestapo searched out the conspirators. By September, files were discovered which incriminated so many that Hitler paused before authorizing the massacre. Bonhoeffer planned an escape. Before the day the plane was to be ready to take him out of the country, he heard that his brother, Klaus, had been arrested. He abandoned the plan and on October 8 he was transferred to the prison in the cellars of the Gestapo headquarters. He remained there for four months.

In the storm of these events (but before the move to Prinz Albrecht Strasse) he wrote this poem. All hope of survival had gone. The prospect of death occupied his mind.

But he could have written this poem at almost any time in his life. It was autobiographical, tracing his own lodgings on the way to freedom, a freedom which could only be fulfilled in death.

Each stanza mirrors a period in his life:

1. DISCIPLINE

He lived and taught the first stanza in 1935, when he returned from England, after giving up his plan to visit Gandhi in order to lead a seminary of the Confessing Church. On September 6, 1935, he drew up a plan for "The Establishment of a Community of Brethren at the Finkenwalde Seminary." It included the following plan and pattern:

> The brethren of the community live together with a strict liturgical ordering of their day. They are guided through the day, not by cultic forms, but by the Word of the Bible and by prayer. They are bound together by brotherly admonition and discipline and by open confession. (*The Way to Freedom,* Collins, 1966, 31)

Those who participated in this community bear witness to the emphasis on discipline—"learn first of all to discipline yourself."

2. ACTION

There is no better example of Bonhoeffer's belief in action than the decision he made to leave the safety of America once the war was inevitable. It was against the advice of his friends, who wished to protect him, but he knew that he could have no part in the rebuilding of church and state in Germany after the war if he was not there during the sufferings of war. He believed that an observer from a safe distance cannot participate in the healing of a nation. At the beginning of July 1939, he wrote to Reinhold Niebuhr,

> I will have no right to participate in the reconstruction of Christian life in Germany after the war if I do not share the trials of this time with my people ... Christians in Germany will face the terrible alternative of either willing the defeat of their nation in order that Christian civilization might survive, or willing the victory of their nation and thereby destroying our civilization. I know which of these alternatives I must choose; but I cannot make that choice in the security of America. (*The Way to Freedom,* 246)

He summarizes this in the poem: "Not in the flight of ideas, but only in action is there freedom."

3. SUFFERING

Once back in Germany, his brother-in-law Hans von Dohnanyi invited him to join the Conspiracy. It was dangerous, but exhilarating. He took a party of Jews to safety in Switzerland, he traveled to neutral and occupied countries on an official passport, and in 1942 he conducted a conversation with the Bishop of Chichester in Sweden, in which he sought the support of the enemies of his country. At this point, he was strong. Then came the arrest and he wrote this poem in the helplessness of prison.

> Only for a moment did you touch the bliss of
> freedom,
> then you gave it back to God that he might
> gloriously fulfill it.

This is a very uncomfortable lodge for the night—suffering. But though "the strong active hands are bound now," he is progressing towards freedom.

4. DEATH

All his life, Bonhoeffer had a strange fascination with death. From his childhood he felt it to be a kind of triumph. Now that the plot had failed and soon the names of the conspirators would be known, there was little chance that he would survive. He faced death before it came, and what he says about death is not the Greek concept of opening the cage of life to let the bird fly free. For him, death is a liberating power, a final step into freedom, a clarifying of vision. In his "Ethics," he understands suicide as the last act of freedom, although he regards it as a denial of faith. Death must come as the climax to a long search for freedom through discipline, action, suffering and, at the last, death: "we see at last what here we could not see."

Johann Christoph Hampe, in his commentary on this poem, has detected a bold theological insight which is quite new, "expressed in words so simple that they cannot fail to move." Attempting to express in his own words what is Bonhoeffer's summary of an entire life, Hampe writes,

One who has stood in "the storm of events" has found the eye of the hurricane where stillness prevails. Talking of death brings joy. The one who is to depart offers guidance. The one who has failed goes to meet his God. Freedom is granted to one who wanted to bring freedom. (Hampe, 73)

At such a time, the decision is made whether human action is a matter of faith or not. Death comes "whether we understand our suffering as an extension of our action and a completion of freedom or not."

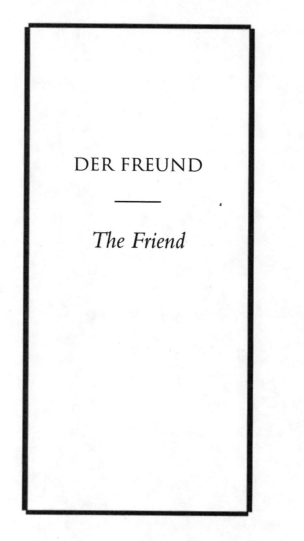

DER FREUND

———

The Friend

DER FREUND—*THE FRIEND*

Not from the hard ground,
where blood and race and binding oath
are sacred and powerful;
where the very earth itself
keeps guard and defends
the consecrated orders of creation
against the madness and frenzy of disorder;
not from the hard ground of the earth,
but freely chosen and desired,
the longing of the spirit,
which neither duty nor law requires,
the friend will offer to the friend.

Beside the nourishing field of corn,
which men faithfully plant and tend,
laboring and sweating in the field,
and, if needs be,
sacrifice their life's blood;
beside the field of daily bread,
those same men also leave
the lovely cornflower to bloom.
No one planted, nor watered it,
defenseless it grows in freedom
and supremely confident
that it will be allowed to live
under the open sky

and undisturbed.
Beside the necessary growth
produced from heavy, earthy work,
beside marriage, work, and the sword,
the unplanned will also
flourish,
and grow towards the sun.

Not only the ripening fruit,
but also flowers are beautiful.
Whether the fruit serves the flower
or the flower the fruit only—
who knows?
Yet both are given to us.
Costly, rare blooms—
sprung from the freedom of the playful,
brave, and trusting spirit
in a happy hour—
such is the friend to the friend.
Playful, at first,
on the far journeys of the spirit,
into wonderful,
distant realms,
which in the haze of the morning sun
glitter like gold;
but in the heat of the day
are by thin clouds in a blue sky
encompassed;

while in the stirrings of the night,
lit only by the lamp,
like hidden private treasures,
they beckon the seeker.

Then when the spirit moves a man
to great, serene, audacious thoughts
of heart and mind,
he may look the world in the face
with clear eyes and open countenance;
then, if action is joined to the spirit
—by which alone it stands or falls—
from this action,
sound and strong,
the work grows,
giving content to thought and meaning
to the life of the man;
then the active, lonely man
longs for
the befriending, understanding spirit of another.
Like a clear, fresh flow of water,
in which the spirit cleanses itself from the dust of
     the day,
cooled from the burning heat,
strengthened in the hour of tiredness—
like a fortress, to which after the dangers of battle
the spirit retires
to find safety, comfort and strength—
such is the friend to the friend.

And the spirit wants to trust,
trust unconditionally.
Disgusted by the worm,
hidden in the shadows of the good,
nourishing itself on envy, scandal and suspicion,
and the poisonous tongues of a nest of vipers,
who fear and hate and vilify
the secret of the free mind,
and of the sincere heart.
The spirit longs to cleanse itself
from all hypocrisy
and trust itself to the other spirit
totally open,
bound to that spirit,
freely and in truth.
Then, ungrudgingly, he will respond,
will praise,
will give thanks,
will find joy and strength
in the other spirit.
Even under severe pressure
and strong rebuke
he willingly submits.
Not by command, nor by alien laws and doctrines,
but by good and earnest counsel,
which liberates,
the mature man seeks
from the true friend.

Far or near
in success and in failure,
the one recognizes in the other
the true helper
towards freedom
and humanity.

Addendum written on the morning of August 28

At the midnight hour, the hideous siren's song,
I thought of you in silence and for long,
how you fare now and how once you were
and that I wish you home for the New Year.

At half past one, the silence ended at last,
I heard the siren's cry, all danger past.
In that I have seen a kindly omen thereby,
that all danger will surely pass you by.

COMMENTARY ON
"Der Freund"

This is an intimate poem, addressed to a specific individual, Eberhard Bethge. Bonhoeffer had many friends, but there were only two to whom he could have addressed this poem: Franz Hildebrandt and Eberhard Bethge. Those two close friendships covered the greater part of his adult life—from his student days to his execution. He was friends with Franz Hildebrandt from 1927 to 1937 and with Eberhard Bethge from 1935 to 1945. The overlapping years, 1935–1937, found all three together. They shared music, theology, and fun with Bonhoeffer, indulging in practical jokes. That period is caught by the lines

> Playful, at first,
> on the far journeys of the spirit,
> into wonderful,
> distant realms,
> which in the haze of the morning sun
> glitter like gold.

This refers to time they spent together in Finkenwalde, and for Franz also the earlier period in London, where Bonhoeffer served his German-speaking congregation and often relaxed with Franz. The Bishop of Chichester called them, "my two boys."

But this poem is a birthday poem for Eberhard. It is the second he wrote for Eberhard that year. The first was the *"Stationen auf dem Wege zur Freihiet,"* which Bethge acknowledges in his letter of August 26, 1944, from the Italian Front:

> You can't give anything more personal than a poem. And you could hardly give me greater joy. There is no greater self-sacrifice, no better way of signifying an otherwise unattainable nearness than in a poem. (LPP, 395)

Bethge did not write about *"Der Freund"* until September 21. Then, he refers to it as "a unique form of birthday celebration."

Of *"Der Freund"* Christoph Hampe has said, "If the previous poem spoke of freedom, here we have freedom itself." Hampe seems to me to have gotten it right. *"Stationen"* described "freedom," as it developed, while *"Der Freund"* described the utter freedom with which a friend could relate most intimately to a friend, without qualifications. Bethge found the fourth stanza difficult.

When the translation of *Letters and Papers from Prison* first appeared in 1953, it was not known who the friend was who received these letters and this intimate poem. When Bethge spoke at a student conference in New Hampshire in 1957–58, the identity of the friend was still unknown. One of the participants asked him if he knew who the recipient of these letters was, because "it must be a homosexual partnership." Bethge replied immediately, "No, we were fairly normal!" and he went on to show that there was no such sexual relationship.

We need to read this poem in the context of the "Prussian Mandates," as Bonhoeffer describes them in his letter of January 23, 1944, to both Renate and Eberhard:

> Marriage, work, state and church all have their definite, divine mandate ... Our "Protestant" (not Lutheran) Prussian work has been so dominated by the four mandates that the sphere of freedom has receded into the background. (LPP, 192–3)

He wonders for a while if the church could provide a place for understanding the "area of freedom," which he identifies as art, education, friendship, and play. In developing this he comments,

> I believe that within the sphere of this freedom is by far the rarest and most priceless treasure ... it cannot be compared with the treasures of the mandates, for in relation to them it is *sui generis;* it belongs to them as the cornflower belongs to the cornfield. (LPP, 197)

In this poem, Bonhoeffer contrasts "friendship" with the "mandates." He describes the mandates as

—the hard ground,
where blood and race and binding oath
are sacred and powerful.

Friendship, on the other hand, he describes as

> —freely chosen and desired,
> the longing of the spirit,
> which neither duty nor law requires.

The mandates are represented by the field of corn:

> which men faithfully plant and tend,
> laboring and sweating in the field.

Friendship, in contrast, he portrays as

> the lovely cornflower . . .
> No one planted, nor watered it,
> defenseless it grows in freedom
> and supremely confident
> that it will be allowed to live
> under the open sky
> and undisturbed.

Bethge confesses that the poem "attracted" him, but asks for a toning down of the "value/judgments"— "Could you omit the 'lovely' in the line 'the lovely cornflower,' as at that point you suddenly move from a continuous viewpoint into a value judgment." He admits that the line "but also flowers are beautiful" is acceptable, yet he finds the phrase "costly, rare blooms" unnecessary. Bethge has one more comment to make about this poem which I have tried to keep in the translation: "The occasional over-short and over-long lines match the very thoughtful content well" (LPP, 396).

The poem ends with a dedication to Eberhard and a sense that he will be preserved from all danger. When Bonhoeffer rhymes, as he does in this addition written on the morning of August 28 (and also in *"Vergangenheit"*), he nearly always has a very personal word to the recipient. Here, it seems that Bonhoeffer is aware of his coming fate, but has a prescience of Bethge's survival.

DER TOD DES MOSE

—

The Death of Moses

DER TOD DES MOSE—*THE DEATH OF MOSES*

On the summit of the mountain stands
Moses, the prophet, in God's hands.

His eyes are steady and his vision clear,
to see the holy, promised land appear.

That he might for his death be ready,
God held his aged servant steady.

On the heights where no one goes,
to him, the promised land God shows.

Spread beneath the wanderer's tired feet,
lies the home he longs to greet,

blessing it with his last breath,
he is prepared in peace for death.

"From afar, you see the saving work of my hand,
but shall not enter, nor treat upon, the promised
     land."

And the old eyes gazed upon the distant sight,
appearing dimly in the morning light.

Clay, molded by God's mighty hand, he was made
a sacrificial vessel. Moses prayed:

"Thus you fulfill what you have spoken,
your word to me was never broken.

Whether your grace or punishment was set,
it always came and must be met.

Once you did in trembling fire ascend.
I was then your chosen and your friend.

Your mouth the source of holiness,
your eyes to see the poorest in lowliness,

your ear to hear your people's cry and plight,
your arm to break the enemy's might,

the back, carrying the weak who could no further
      go,
and destroying the anger of friend and foe,

the mediator of your people as their prayers ascend
I was your instrument, Lord, your prophet and your
      friend.

Therefore you send me death on this steep
      mountain side,
not in the depths where lesser men have died,

the death with clear vision and distant sight,
of the commander, who led his people in the fight,

beyond the gloomy limits of the dying
already the signs of new times espying.

When now the shades of death o'ercome me
your salvation fulfilled from afar I see.

Holy Land, to me you have appeared,
like a bejewelled bride, lovely and endeared,

the bridal dress lights up your virgin face,
your bridal jewels are of costly grace.

Let these old eyes so oft betrayed,
drink in your sweet loveliness displayed.

Let this life, before its powers shrink,
once more from the streams of joy drink.

God's Land, before your doors open wide
we stand, lost in a dream, no joy denied.

The blessing of the patriarchs we feel already
blowing towards us, full of promise and steady.

God's Vineyard, moistened by the dew in the early
    hour,
bunches of grapes, nourished and cradled by the
    sun's power,

God's Garden, where your fruits swell
and clear water gushes from your well,

God's Grace, flowing over a free earth,
to a holy and new people will give birth.

God's Law will protect both strong and weak
from those who by tyranny and force the mastery
    seek.

God's Truth will guide from human learning
and erring people, to faith returning.

God's Peace will, like strong towers,
hearts, houses, cities protect with its powers.

God's Rest will on his faithful people fall
like a great celebration at his call.

And a peaceful people on simple lines
will plough the earth and plant the vines,

and each will call the other brother,
proud hearts burn not with envy of another,

and boys by their fathers will be told
to honor the sacred and respect the old,

and girls will be beautiful and dutiful and pure,
the people's joy and honor and adornment to
      endure.

Those who once ate the strangers' bread
will not therefore leave the stranger dead.

On the orphan, the poor and the widow,
the righteous man will freely his care bestow.

God who dwelt among our fathers in the past,
let our sons be prayerful people to the last!

In high festival, may this to thy glory
lead the people up to holiness by sacred story.

To you, Lord, we will the offering bring,
and to you the songs of salvation sing.

In thanks and rejoicing with one voice,
may your people proclaim they are your choice.

The world is great; it stretches to the sky,
people behold, as they in deep confusion lie.

In your Word, which you to us make known,
to all peoples you have the way to life now shown.

Always, the world will in days of heavy task,
of your holy ten commandments ask.

Always, a people, however guilty they be,
alone in your holiness will healing see.

And thus my people are called with attractions fair,
to the free land and the free air.

Possess the mountains and the fertile lands,
blessed by your fathers' godly hands,

wipe from their brows the hot desert sand
and breathe freedom in the promised land.

Awake, take hold, it is no mirage you have dreamed,
God has the tired hearts redeemed.

Look at the glory of the promised land and see
all is yours and you are set free."

On the summit of the mountain stands
Moses, the prophet, in God's hands.

His eyes are steady and his vision clear,
to see the holy, promised land appear.

"Thus you fulfill what you have spoken,
your word to me you have never broken.

Your grace saves and delights,
but your anger disowns and smites.

Faithful Lord, your servant faithless in distrust,
but knowing well: you are forever just.

So enforce your punishment today,
take me in the log sleep of death away.

Of the holy land's fruitful vine,
untarnished faith alone may drink the wine.

Out of the house of bondage have you set us free
that we your belovéd children might be.

Through raging waters and desert land
wonderfully have you led us by the hand;

the people's grumbles, complaints, and scorn,
with patience you have graciously borne.

Not by kindness only have they learned in those
    days
the stubborn paths of faith and triumphant praise,

when they lusted after idols to your face,
instead of feeding upon the bread of your grace,

until your anger with plague and deadly snake
great gaps among your people make.

The future heirs of the promised land
fell like outcast rebels in the sand.

In the midst of their wandering way,
in your fury, you cast them away.

You sought for one the multitude through;
one that was faithful and true,

but all those who swore to be true
when the sea of reeds your power knew,

departed from you in their hearts
and left their bodies in desert parts.

Those you led to their salvation
have risen against you, a rebel nation.

Of this generation, once your delight,
not one remained true to you and right.

When you rejected the elders with scorn,
when a new generation was born,

and now when the young like the old in their day
scoff at your word and from you turn away,

Lord you know, in the course of the years,
a careless word from me reached your ears.

Doubting and impatient thought
almost brought my faith to nought.

You forgive; but 'tis a blazing fire
to stand before the Truth, a liar.

Your nearness and of your face the sight
are to the penitent, a wounding light.

Your sadness and your great scorn
bury into my flesh, a deadly thorn.

Before your holy word, which you inflamed,
that which I preached, I am ashamed.

He who has tasted the fruit of doubt,
from God's table is shut out.

From the holy land's fruitful vine,
untarnished faith alone can drink the wine.

You allow me no escape, Lord, from your
     punishment,
but favor me with death on this high battlement.

Pour for the doubter the bitter draft of his ways,
and let faith along speak thanks and praise.

Wonderfully have you dealt with me,
blends of bitterness and sweet to see,

let me through the veil of death behold
my people at their festival bold.

God, into your eternities going,
I see my people march with freedom glowing.

You who punish sin and forgive readily,
God, you know I have loved this people steadily.

That I have borne their shame and sacrifice
and seen their salvation—will suffice.

Hold, support me, I lose my stave,
faithful God, prepare me for my grave."

COMMENTARY ON
"Der Tod des Mose"

Bonhoeffer wrote to Bethge that he had taken the death of Moses as a theme for his work, but that he had to work "in verse," otherwise it would be too explosive! On September 30, 1944, Bethge acknowledged the poem, which he had received the day before. His comments were that "It moved me very much, but I'm not sure what to make of it. The language is fine, but with the fetters of the rhyme, it didn't seem quite like your other things." He makes no suggestions for alterations, but adds, "I find your thoughts about the future bold and perhaps even comforting." There was no further correspondence between the two friends after that—at least, none that has survived (LPP, 398).

When Bethge compiled *Wilerstand und Ergbung,* which in English has the title *Letters and Papers from Prison,* he did not include this poem. Although it appeared in German in several other publications, including the *Gesammelte Schriften,* only part of it has been translated into English before. A part of the poem was translated by John Bowden and included in the English version of J. C. Hampe's book *Prayers from Prison* (pp. 33–34). That translation has the fine quality that all of John Bowden's translations have, but it is only a part of this long poem, and it has not retained the rhyme.

Clearly, Bethge thought the rhyme was a mistake and Bowden appears to agree with him. I am convinced that Bonhoeffer had a reason for fettering himself with the rhyme and have therefore undertaken the tiresome task of also fettering myself with it because I think it does something for our understanding of Bonhoeffer at this crucial time.

At the end of September, incriminating documents of the *Abwehr* (military intelligence) with which many of the Bonhoeffer family were linked were discovered at Zossen. A whole series of arrests began and the family was under grave threat. Bonhoeffer and his guard had planned an escape in great detail for early in October, but Dietrich refused to go through with it because of the danger it would bring to his family whether or not he succeeded. This was the period when he finished this poem. Since the failure of the July Plot, he had been fairly sure that if he did not escape, he would certainly be executed. His uncle—General Von Hase—had already been hanged.

Working on the account of the death of Moses in Deuteronomy, he could not fail to identify with the ancient prophet. After having led his people through the wilderness and seen them all die on the way, Moses had to face the fact that he himself would not be allowed to enter the Promised Land—only a new generation with faith and hope in the future would enter. In New York, in 1939, Bonhoeffer had written to say that he must cancel all the lectures arranged to keep him safe in America and return home. This was like the call of Moses from the security of Midian to the dangers of Pharaoh's Egypt where he was a wanted man. Like Moses, Bonhoeffer had his time of triumph. In Sweden with Bell in 1942, he was full of hope as the conspiracy gained support in Germany. Even then, however, he knew that his country must suffer for what they had done. As Moses was disappointed with the wavering faith of the people he led in the wilderness, Bonhoeffer was disappointed with his church which was content to survive until the evil times were over, concerned only with "Self-preservation, as though that were an end in itself." As the people in the wilderness lost sight of the vision, so the church in Germany, he said, had lost its power to proclaim the gospel of forgiveness and reconciliation to the world. He had his moments when, like Moses, he was weary of his vacillating church. We can hear his own experience in the following lines:

> You sought just one of the multitude through;
> one that was faithful and true,
>
> but all those who swore to be true
> when the sea of reeds your power knew,
>
> departed from you in their hearts
> and left their bodies in desert parts.

Bonhoeffer had no doubt about the justice of God: "Thus you fulfill what you have spoken, your word to me was never broken."

The tension of the ideas in these lines is held in check by the rhyme, as Bonhoeffer well knew. This is even more evident when he compares his own period of failure and doubt with that of Moses, whose failure brought him the terrible punishment of not entering the Promised Land he had led the people to. Bonhoeffer often reemphasizes the sadness of Moses, which was like his own deep disappointment as it became clear that he would not survive to play his part in the reconstruction of Christian life after the war in Germany. This led him to write a summary of a book he wanted to write to guide the church into the future.

Almost fifteen years earlier, in 1930, during the Christmas break in his studies at Union Theological Seminary, New York, Bonhoeffer and his friend Erwin Sutz visited Cuba. There he met his old governess Käthe Horn, who was teaching in Havana. He inspected her school and preached later on the text of the death of Moses (Deuteronomy 32:48–52). He had been deeply troubled by the effects of the Great Depression in America—hunger, long lines of the unemployed, and hopelessness among the black population. He knew of the situation in Germany but felt also the suffering of children throughout the world, the starving in China, the oppressed in India. All this made it hard to celebrate

Christmas lightly. In that sermon he asks the question why Moses had to die before the Promised Land. His answer is: "The sinner dies before the Promised Land. Moses belongs to his people, therefore he dies." And so he ends this poem fifteen years later:

> You who punish sin and forgive readily,
> God, you know I have loved this people steadily.
>
> That I have borne their shame and sacrifice
> and seen their salvation—will suffice.
>
> Hold, support me, I lose my stave,
> faithful God, prepare me for my grave.

Bethge was confused by this poem, although deeply moved. He also sensed that Bonhoeffer's view of the future—for Germany, if not for himself—was "bold and perhaps even comforting."

Whether Bonhoeffer speaks of the Hebrews approaching the Promised Land, or, as in a sermon to young people, when he speaks of the Christian's Promised Land, he sees always both life and death. Hence the three couplets before that last quote:

> Wonderfully have you dealt with me,
> blends of bitterness and sweet to see,

let me through the veil of death behold
my people at their festival bold.

God, into your eternities going,
I see my people march with freedom glowing.

These lines show Bonhoeffer's belief that there would
be a future for Germany.

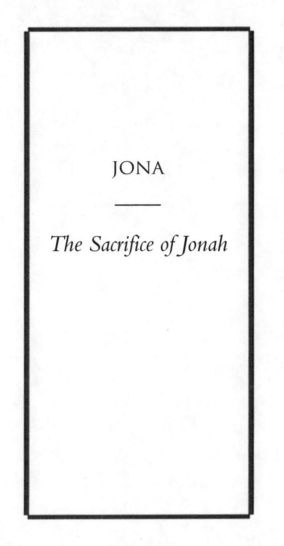

JONA

———

The Sacrifice of Jonah

JONA—THE SACRIFICE OF JONAH

In face of death they screamed and strained
to hold the soaking ropes, creaking in the wind,
and wild scenes appeared, in full horror, behind
the sea's tumultuous waves and forces unrestrained.

"You gods eternal, ever good, who now offense
    betoken,
save us, or give a sign that we may know
who with secret sins has made you so:
murderer, blasphemer, or one whose oath is broken,

one, whose hidden wrongs have brought us to this
    evil,
that his pride might profit as best it can!"
Thus they prayed and Jonah spoke, "I am the man!
My life is forfeit. I opposed God's will."

"Cast me out, my guilt incurs God's anger still.
The righteous should not perish with wrong!"
They trembled, but their hands were strong
to drop the guilty. And now the sea was still!

COMMENTARY ON
"Jona"

This was the last of Bonhoeffer's poems to be written in Cell 92, at the prison he had known for eighteen months. His situation was soon to change and he was aware of that.

The poem deals with one small, but crucial incident in the life of the prophet Jonah. The prophet had been told to go eastward to Nineveh, where he was to preach repentance lest a terrible fate befall the city. Jonah did not want Nineveh to repent and be forgiven. He wanted that evil city to be destroyed. He therefore took a boat, not eastward, but westward towards Spain. He opposed God's will consciously.

The ship ran into a violent storm and the seamen were terrified by its force. The story is told in twelve verses in the Bible, beginning, "The sailors were afraid, and each cried out to his god for help . . ." They find Jonah asleep and ask him to call upon his god for help. They then cast lots and when they discover that the cause of the storm is Jonah, they ask him what they should do. He replies, "Take me and throw me overboard." At first they try to row for the shore, but at last, "They took Jonah and threw him overboard, and the sea stopped raging."

Moses and Jonah became symbolic figures for Bonhoeffer. In Moses, he sees a servant of God punished for his lack of faith. Bonhoeffer's Bible is marked in several places, underlining the Moses story in Exodus, Numbers, and Leviticus. He notes that Moses is not sacrificed for his nation, and there is one point in the poem at which this is touched upon. God molds him like clay into a sacrificial vessel and Moses prays. But this Bonhoeffer knows is not central to the biblical story.

With Jonah, the sacrifice is clear. Just as Jonah had refused to go to Nineveh for its salvation, so he is sacrificed at the end of the poem for people who are not Jews, but who worship other gods. There is a progression in his thinking between these two poems.

Bonhoeffer moves from punishment for his guilt—the sacrifice of his righteousness (*"Nächtliche Stimmen"* brings this out)—to see that his death, like the death of many others after the failure of the July Plot, is for the salvation of Germany. If we put *"Nächtliche Stimmen"* side by side with *"Jona,"* we can hear the relevance of the cry, "I am the man! My life is forfeit." At times, he must also have added, "I opposed God's will." In *"Jona"* there is a "confession."

The poem was sent to Maria with the request that she copy it for Eberhard and send it to him without saying who it was from—Eberhard would know. He expected Eberhard to understand *"Jona,"* but to Maria he writes, "You may find it a trifle incomprehensible." I don't think she did.

In his two volume edition of Bonhoeffer's *Sermons* Otto Dudzus perceived that "In the Jonah poem, Bonhoeffer expresses the extreme aspect of his confrontation with death." After relating this to the abandoned escape plan for the sake of his family he adds:

> Thus he offers his life for the others. But there is a more profound sense in which he describes the setting of this sacrifice:
>
> > In face of death they screamed and strained
> > to hold the soaking ropes, creaking in the wind,
> > and wild scenes appeared in full horror behind
> > the sea's tumultuous wave and forces unrestrained.
>
> What else can Bonhoeffer mean than the situation of the war and of the inner, chaotic state of his people, with all the fear, the flights into illusion and above all the consciousness of guilt? "Cast me out!" he says at this moment and brings to fulfilment what has long been a strong motif in his thinking, preaching and action, namely: In his own search for the guilty in order to separate himself from them, he finds himself to be the guilty one. It is in this sense that he understands confession, conversion and discipleship. (Dudzus, I., 91)

There was next a change. Bonhoeffer was moved to the Gestapo cellars and felt ready to compose his last poem. In anticipation he wrote a covering letter for *"Jona"* to Maria, which was quite simple but profound:

Dear Maria, thank you for all your loyalty, courage and confidence! That's our prime requirement. I'm immensely proud of you and all of you. The reading for today (Job 5:12: He frustrates the devices of the crafty, so that their hands achieve no success) is very fine. Love to my parents and my brothers and sisters. I'm always with you [plural] in my thoughts. I kiss you tenderly. (LLC 92, 225)

That simple note has significance also for the next poem—these family and friends are the kindly powers of which he will write in the Gestapo cellar after October 8, 1944.

VON GUTEN
MÄCHTEN

---

*By Kindly Powers
Surrounded*

Von guten Mächten—By Kindly Powers Surrounded

1. By kindly powers surrounded, peaceful and true,
wonderfully protected with consolation dear,
safely, I dwell with you this whole day through,
and surely into another year.

2. Though from the old our hearts are still in pain,
while evil days oppress with burdens still,
Lord, give to our frightened souls again,
salvation and thy promises fulfill.

3. And shouldst thou offer us the bitter cup,
    resembling
sorrow, filled to the brim and overflowing,
we will receive it thankfully, without trembling,
from thy hand, so good and ever-loving.

4. But if it be thy will again to give
joy of this world and bright sunshine,
then in our minds we will past times relive
and all our days be wholly thine.

5. Let candles burn, both warm and bright,
which to our darkness thou has brought,
and, if that can be, bring us together in the light,
thy light shines in the night unsought.

6. When we are wrapped in silence most profound,
may we hear that song most fully raised
from all the unseen world that lies around
and thou art by all thy children praised.

7. By kindly powers protected wonderfully,
confident, we wait for come what may.
Night and morning, God is by us, faithfully
and surely at each new born day.

COMMENTARY ON
"Von guten Mächten"

This last poem is the most popular of them all, learned by heart by many a German child and most easily transposed into a hymn. It is a Gethsemane prayer—"Lord, if it be possible, let this cup pass from me," and, "Nevertheless, thy will not mine be done."

It was written in the Gestapo cellar of Prinz Albrecht Strasse, where conditions were harsh—"It's hell in here," Admiral Canaris said to Bonhoeffer when they met in the communal washroom. Many of those involved in the conspiracy were in the cells there, including Maria's cousin, Fabian von Schlabrendorff, who gave the little information we have of Bonhoeffer's activities during this period. These included some very clever antics he pulled in order to speak with his brother-in-law, Hans von Dohnanyi, so that they might agree to what each would say under interrogation. Von Dohnanyi also tells of Bonhoeffer's attitude to all around him:

> He was always cheerful, always consistently friendly and obliging, with the result that—to my surprise— it did not take him long to captivate psychologically the guards, who were far from brimming over with the milk of human kindness. (LLC 92, 226)

There was still a faint hope of survival and, as the war seemed almost over, the hope that it would end before they were all executed. After about two months conditions were relaxed a bit and Bonhoeffer was able to write a Christmas letter to Maria. That letter, dated December 19,1944, conveys love and greetings to parents and friends. It also contains a comment on the "kindly powers," which in the poem surround him, "peaceful and true," which "wonderfully protected" him.

> I sense my connection with you all. It's as if, in solitude, the soul develops organs of which we're hardly aware in everyday life. So I haven't for an instant felt lonely and forlorn. You yourself, my parents, all of you including my friends and students on active service—are my constant companions. Your prayers and kind thoughts, passages from the Bible, long forgotten conversations, pieces of music, books—all are invested with life and reality as never before. I live in a great unseen realm of whose real existence I'm in no doubt. (LLC 92, 227)

He uses the plural *"euch"* in such lines as "I dwell with *you* this whole day through," whereas the singular *"Du"* is used only of God, and thus I have translated "you" and "thou" to make the distinction.

The passage I have just quoted in the letter is in particular a comment upon the penultimate stanza:

When we are wrapped in silence most profound,
may we hear that song most fully raised

from all the unseen world which lies around
and thou art by all thy children praised.

The poem was sent with that letter, and with this
comment:

> Here are another few verses that have occurred to me
> in recent nights. They're my Christmas greetings to you,
> my parents and my brothers and sisters. (LLC 92, 228)

On January 12, the Russians broke through the German
defenses and Maria's home in Pätzig was under threat.
The children were sent westward and eventually her
mother also left. Maria remained in Berlin so that she
might visit Prinz Albrecht Strasse. Bonhoeffer wrote to
his parents on January 17, but soon the prisoners were
moved because of advancing troops from east and west.
Maria went in search of him and even came to Flossenbürg, where seven weeks after she made inquiries about
him, he was executed.

It was on April 9, 1945, that he was offered the "bitter cup" in Flossenbürg, and "received it thankfully, without trembling."

Fabian von Schlabrendorff spoke to Bonhoeffer on
February 7 for the last time. He learned later of how
Bonhoeffer met his end and wrote:

> When after several months I returned to my home (in
> Pätzig) . . . at first saw nothing but rubble. Anything
> that the bombs had spared had been stolen. Only one

book lay undamaged among the bricks and mortar: Dietrich Bonhoeffer's *Nachfolge* [the English title is *The Cost of Discipleship,* but the German bears the meaning of emulating the way of his Master].

Although *By Kindly Powers Surrounded* has been turned into a hymn in many countries and languages, it is not a hymn, but is a prayer of thanksgiving and petition. The thanksgiving is for the "kindly powers" that have surrounded him all his life—family, friends, colleagues, etc; the petition, as has been noted above, is the Gethsemane prayer that the cup may be taken from him. To the end, Dietrich Bonhoeffer emulated his Master.